Christmas Cats in Hats
Grown Up Coloring Book

Dale McSwain

Copyright © 2017 Dale McSwain

www.stelleriabooks.com

All rights reserved.

ISBN: **1539806103**
ISBN-13: **978-1539806103**

For
Sherrie, Sarah, Jeramie, Aubrie
And Little Everly Lane

And Speedy the Cat

"Nothing makes a house cozier than a cat ." – Gladys Taber

Consider how the wild flowers grow. They do not labor or spin. Yet I tell you not even Solomon in all his splendor was dressed as one of these.
Luke 12:27

CONTENTS

Christmas Cat in Hat With Presents

Hidden Flower is Tall Chiming Bell

Christmas Cat in a Hat Under a Tree

Hidden Flower is Globe Flower

Sleepy Christmas Cat in a Hat in a Chair

Hidden Flower is American Bistort

Very Happy Christmas Cat in a Hat

Hidden Flower is Mountain Iris

Christmas Cat Inside of a Hat

Hidden Flower is Globe Flower

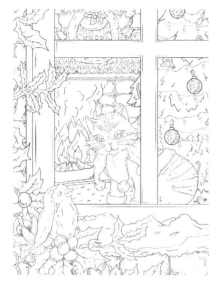

Christmas Cat Eyeing a Snow Bird

Hidden Flower is Globe Flower

Christmas Cat in a Window

Hidden Flower is Tall Chiming Bell

Christmas Cat in a Hat in a Stocking

Hidden Flower is Alpine Forget Me Not

Christmas Cat in a Hat in a Chair

Hidden Flower is Alpine Sunflower

Christmas cat in a Hat in a Shop

Hidden Flower is Globe Flower

Christmas cat in a Hat on A Shelf

Hidden Flower is Indian Paintbrush

Christmas Cat in a Hat on a Chair

Hidden Flower is Alpine Forget Me Not

Christmas Cat in A Hat on A Bench

Hidden Flower is Globe Flower

Christmas Cat On a Piano

Hidden Flower is Many Flower Stickseed

Christmas Cat in a Hat in A Trunk

Hidden Flower is Tall Chiming Bell

Christmas Cat in a Hat in Bed

Hidden flower is Alpine Sunflower

Christmas Cat in a Hat on A Mantel

Hidden Flower is Tall Chiming Bell

Christmas Cat in a Hat Over a Fire

Hidden Flower is Alpine Sunflower

Christmas Cat in a Hat On a Stair

Hidden Flower is Glacier Lily

Christmas Cat in a Hat Under a Tree

Hidden Flower is Shooting Star

I hope you find this book enjoyable. Stelleria Books was born on wildflowers and this book has a little hidden gem that you will love. Each Christmas scene has a hidden flower from our soon to be released Rocky Mountain Wildflower Coloring Book. There is an index of flowers that you can color in the rear of the book. Watch our website for a release date. Please find us on Facebook and share your thoughts or just say Hi. You might also like our first book Wildflowers of the Smoky Mountains Adult Coloring Book. You can find it on Amazon.

www.stelleriabooks.com
www.facebook.com/stelleriabooks/

Dale McSwain
Stelleria Books
November, 2017

Artwork By:
Completed On:

Artwork By:
Completed On:

Artwork By:
Completed On:

Artwork By:
Completed On:

Artwork By:
Completed On:

Artwork By:
Completed On:

Artwork By:
Completed On:

Artwork By:
Completed On:

Artwork By:
Completed On:

Artwork By:
Completed On:

Artwork By:
Completed On:

Artwork By:
Completed On:

Artwork By:

Completed On:

Artwork By:
Completed On:

Artwork By:
Completed On:

Artwork By:
Completed On:

Artwork By:
Completed On:

Artwork By:

Completed On:

Artwork By:
Completed On:

Artwork By:
Completed On:

Indian Paintbrush

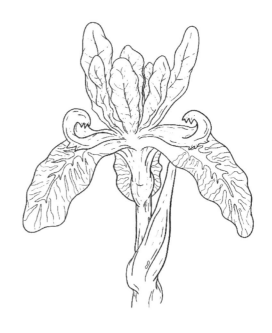
Mountain Iris

Alpine Forget Me Not

Tall Chiming Bell

Alpine Forget Me Not   Alpine Sunflower

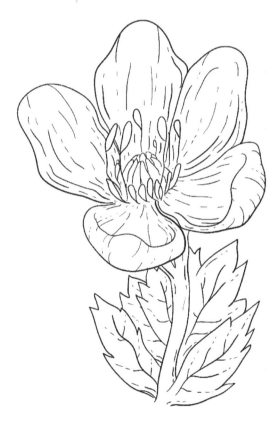

American Bistort   Globeflower

Made in the USA
Las Vegas, NV
26 October 2023